MW00563225

IMAGES
of America

RUSSELL CITY

Barbara Russell, great-great granddaughter of Joel and Carrie Russell, for whom the area came to be named, was born and raised in Hayward. She is seen here with the family heirloom portrait of Maud Faulkner Russell, her great-great aunt who was the daughter of Joel and Carrie. (Author's collection.)

ON THE COVER: Pictured are the Russell Public School champions of the 1946 Hayward Recreation Games. Proudly holding their victory banner are members of the winning eighth-grade team. (Courtesy of Hayward Area Historical Society.)

IMAGES
of America

RUSSELL CITY

María Ochoa with the
Hayward Area Historical Society

ARCADIA
PUBLISHING

Published by Arcadia Publishing
Charleston, South Carolina

Library of Congress Control Number: 2009921930

For all general information contact Arcadia Publishing at:
Telephone 843-853-2070
Fax 843-853-0044
E-mail sales@arcadiapublishing.com
For customer service and orders:
Toll-Free 1-888-313-2665

Visit us on the Internet at www.arcadiapublishing.com

*For all the people who were stewards of this
land and appreciated its splendor.*

CONTENTS

ACKNOWLEDGMENTS

Many thanks are due to the hundreds of people who made this pictorial history of Russell City possible. First always is my family, who provide love and encouragement so that I may work as a writer. My husband, Mike Sweeney, endures endless takeout and missed appointments, and still he smiles and loves me. Christine V., Christine C., Sue, Joe, and Sue's Mike are all good-natured about my endless chatter regarding this work. For other times when the process grows difficult, Lord Ganesh guides me through these moments. The Hayward Area Historical Society is a gem of a cultural institution, and the entire staff deserves high praise for their commitment to local history. Former executive director Jim DeMersman supported an early iteration of this project, and Myron Freedman has continued that legacy of support. Diane Curry is a phenomenal historian, curator, writer, and all-around exceptional professional. Without Diane, this book would be a much less polished work. Heather Mellon and Marcess Owings were wonderfully good-natured about their assistance. The Creative Work Fund supported our collaboration with a 2001 artists grant. The funds allowed me to interview more than 22 former residents. Kelly Reed is patient beyond belief and offered useful editorial counsel in her work as editor for Arcadia Publishing. Photographs not provided by the Hayward Area Historical Society came from Connie Anderson; Jan Chandler Hunter; James and Priscilla Figueroa; Loretta Horat Machado; Mildred Jean Hill-Eddens; William Mette; Sam and Juanita Nava; Barbara Russell; Dorothy Tolefree-Babbitt; Karen Verili; and Norman Zimmerman, as well as the Bancroft Library, University of California, Berkeley; and the Mark Weber Jazz Collection, University of California, Los Angeles, Performing Arts Special Collection. Unless otherwise noted, images are from the Hayward Area Historical Society.

FOREWORD

I really believe that was holy land out there.
Anybody that was raised out there had it pretty good.

—Joe Harris (grew up in Russell City)

In his novel *Invisible Cities*, Italian writer Italo Calvino imagined Marco Polo with the difficult task of recounting for Genghis Khan the many cities he visited in his travels throughout the ruler's territories, as Khan wished to better understand the places that made up his far-flung empire. Put on the spot, and with no written accounts to give the impatient and imperious emperor, Polo recalls cities in dimensions shaped not by topography, climate, or distance, but by dreams, desires, ambition, and love— a geography of the senses. Marco Polo paints images of past places and people from memory and Khan comes to understand his kingdom as more than so many conquered lands, as places invested with human activity and invention. In this case, memory itself is the book of history.

So it is with the history of Russell City, a place so completely transformed by urban change that hardly a physical trace of it still exists, though it lives and breathes in the vivid memories of those who lived there and in the photographs gathered from their own scrapbooks, shoeboxes, and refrigerator doors. The images tell of a unique community: diverse faces in class photographs during the time of Jim Crow, a woman pitching in to make dirt roads passable, men still marrying machinery and animals to work the farm in a not too distant past. But it is the memories of Russell City residents themselves that bring the story of their community to life. The memories are as fresh as yesterday: of large families growing up packed in small homes, never connected to the basic services most of us take for granted; of walking or driving the unpaved streets to get home, or to school, or past the rank hog farm to the junkyard to buy or sell; or of listening to the thumping music coming from the local night spot fading into the church choir's ringing voices—the same voices, and in the same place, tavern to tabernacle.

All of us grow up shaped by the place we live in, and should we leave, we may return to find that it is still there, if much changed. But for many others, the story is like that of Russell City, a once heralded urban development whose fortunes were transformed as promises went unmet. Like Chavez Ravine in Los Angeles, the great Bronzeville neighborhood in Chicago, or Mill Valley in St. Louis, communities that were home to thousands but were gradually claimed by the surrounding city for train tracks, freeways, and industrial zones or cleared away to simply make the land more attractive for investors. Often voices rose up in protest over such invasive urban actions, even as the people moved away to rebuild homes and lives elsewhere. Historians have been scrambling for decades to piece together the stories of these ephemeral communities that allowed vast numbers of Americans to stake out their lives, either as new or migrating Americans, or simply as participants in a jumble of civic and economic growth spurts, before they or their children moved on. In the hurly-burly that was the American 20th century, it would have been the exception for such places to take the time to even carelessly document such a community, let alone create an archive. In the absence of a strong historic record, the very old technique of using oral history to preserve eyewitness accounts has become a significant modern tool for historians looking at these places, especially when illustrated by personal snapshots.

In the case of Russell City, these events are relatively recent, within the last 50 years, and when the end came, it also came with relative swiftness. During the 1960s, amid debates over annexation and zoning, Russell City homes began to mysteriously burn down, several a night at times. Luckily, if not just as mysteriously, no one was injured from the fires, but the question of the community's future seemed to go up in smoke. As resident Sam Nava commented years later, "I always thought that once it went down, that was it. Nobody would ever remember it again."

Nava hadn't counted on historian and author María Ochoa, who grew up in Hayward and recalls visiting Russell City as a child to attend Spanish-language mass. Years ago, she embarked on a journey to document Russell City through the oral histories of people who lived there, worked there, or like her have vivid memories of going there. Attending annual Russell City reunions and working with the Hayward Area Historical Society, she has been able to gather from the scattered living residents the many photographs that tell the story and also their voices. Her sensitive approach to the people who recalled for her the substance of her narrative, coupled with the images from their lives and times, has given us an extraordinary look at that most elusive of historical topics, ordinary life.

It is a tricky business to capture the past. However, when the canvas of history has been wiped away, it is an amazing feat. María Ochoa's work is a testament and a record to the importance of capturing people's memories while the smells and sounds still emanate from the photographs of a disappeared place, a place that can now be better known by all of us through the geography of their senses.

— Myron Freedman
Executive Director
Hayward Area Historical Society

INTRODUCTION

Seeking Russell City is as elusive as looking for El Dorado, and it is a story that is as uniquely Californian as was the search for a golden city. Known by many names—Rancho San Lorenzo, Russell's, Russell, the Russell District, Little Copenhagen, and Russell City—including those unknown yet used by the Yrgin Ohlones who originally lived on the land, the area was and still is quite beautiful in its natural state. The resources that abounded—clean water, plentiful wildlife, and an abundance of edible vegetation—made the area an attractive site to live.

Gold fever infected hundreds of thousands who traveled from all corners of the world, first to San Francisco and then to mining camps in the foothills of Northern California. One such forty-niner was a New England schoolteacher by the name of Joel Russell, who traveled "round the Cape" and arrived in 1850 just in time to celebrate the state's admission into the Union. Like so many who came hopeful yet unskilled in mining, Russell was not successful. In 1853, the verdant and seemingly unused land near the eastern shore of the bay, in the area that is now Hayward, seemed to Russell a good place to rebuild his life. The Soto family owned the land upon which he squatted. In 1856, the Soto family sold Russell a portion of the rancho. Russell thrived as a farmer growing grains and hay, and eventually he became a major figure in the development of the area. He married Caroline "Carrie" Maria Bartlett, the daughter of a local farming family, and together they raised a daughter, Maud, and two sons, Thomas and Frederick.

Russell sold 700 acres of his bayside property to Danish families—Nielsen, Nygren, Pestdorf, Christiansen, Hansen, and others—newly immigrated to the region, and that area became known as Little Copenhagen. Russell died in 1888 and Carrie in 1903, and their sons, Thomas and Frederick, divided the real estate holdings. "The ranch," as the property by the bay was known within the family, went to Frederick, and the downtown property located where Russell Street now runs became Thomas's. Although an attorney by training, Frederick supported his family as a dairy farmer and nursed a grand vision for his bayside property. In 1906, he began working with a group of real estate investors, the East Shore and Suburban Real Estate Company, who sought to transform the rural area into a thriving metropolis composed of homes whose lavishness would be unsurpassed in the east bay. The recent earthquake that had devastated San Francisco gave the developers hope that displaced residents would choose to move and live in this new city by the bay. By April 1907, maps were drawn up, the land subdivided, and the development was officially designated as Russell City. However, the people who left San Francisco came not to Russell City but to already established areas like Oakland and San José. Further, the economic climate of the time did not generate the sale of much property. An economic depression hit the United States in 1910, shortly after the startup of the development, and momentum was lost. Two decades later, the Great Depression finalized the demise of the project.

Although the metropolitan character of the community was never realized, the rural setting continued to attract migrants and immigrants. At the start of the 20th century, the Horat and Camenzind families established dairies and were joined by immigrants from Europe such as the Zimmermans, who hailed from Germany by way of Pennsylvania. Spanish families, such as the Mateos and Liranzos, also arrived during this period and were at first successful vegetable, fruit, and poultry farmers and later became entrepreneurs in commercial ventures. The Gavellos and the Santuccis, who were of Italian heritage, also came to live in Russell City. One family had a tradition of working the railroad and the other for the hog farm that grew into a noxiously smelly but thriving enterprise. By the 1920s, at least 75 percent of California farm laborers were of Mexican descent. Some like Ernesto Nava became accomplished trade workers in the construction industry. Others like Joe Cota moved from working the fields to well-paying union jobs in automobile manufacturing. African Americans arrived during the Second Great Migration that began in 1940. Families like the Brooks, Eddens, Hills, Simmons, Stones, and Tolefrees hearkened from the states of Louisiana, Texas, and Arkansas. It was during the 1940s and 1950s that the population of Russell City grew rapidly, and the largest numbers of residents were no longer Danes and Germans but Mexicans and African Americans. One reason why so many people from these two ethnic groups resided in Russell City is that nearby communities such as San Leandro, Hayward, and San Lorenzo had covenants that prevented the sale of homes to people who were not white.

While the economic stature of Russell City residents was never great, social riches abounded in the religious traditions and cultural practices of the community. No fewer than seven churches of various denominations—Apostolic, Baptist, Evangelical, Pentecostal, and Roman Catholic—existed in the center of town. Because the various congregations were not wealthy, the places of worship were modest; however, the membership of each church was vibrant. The number of Spanish-speaking residents was numerous in Russell City, and as a result, many of the churches offered bilingual services. Each church had at least one choir, and some congregations organized as many as four different choirs—one each for children, youth, women, and men. Instruments abounded, and banjos, guitars, pianos, organs, violins, saxophones, and flutes accompanied the vocalists. In addition, guest musicians and vocalists were frequently found at Sunday services. It was not unusual for someone who had performed on a Saturday night in one of the Russell City clubs to be found the next morning sharing his or her musical talents in church.

Russell City developed a blues tradition that grew from African Americans whose Southern roots influenced the music that the town came to be known for. It is said that on Saturday nights, songs that pulsed from the clubs invariably included the words "my sweet baby" as music and audiences spilled into the streets of Russell City. On Sunday mornings, those same streets would be filled with worshipful congregants and church music whose lyrics called out to "my sweet Jesus." Notable persons who passed through the town and performed at the clubs included musicians Ray Charles, Big Mama Thornton, and Lowell Fulson. Heavyweight champion boxer Max Baer visited nightspots with names like Miss Al's Night Club (also known as Miss Alve's) and the Russell City Country Club. Baer knew the community well because as a teenager he had lived with his family on a farm located just outside of Russell City near the intersection of the streets now called West Winton Avenue and Hesperian Boulevard.

By the mid-20th century, the population had grown from less than 100 residents to slightly more than 1,000. For all of the grand plans initially envisioned for the community, the residents lived without the infrastructure that was common to those living in nearby cities—water for indoor use, a sewage and rainstorm system, electric and gas utilities, garbage collection, fire protection, police protection, vector and vermin abatement, street lighting, and recreational facilities. In 1954, the residents petitioned the County of Alameda to form the Russell City Community Services District. They were permitted to embark on the establishment of the district, but the funds necessary to the accomplishment of their infrastructure goals were never realized.

In the late 1950s, plans were made by Alameda County and the City of Hayward to designate the area a redevelopment district, acquire the land, evict the residents and businesses, and construct an industrial park. Over time, all of this was accomplished, and the town was no longer. An annual reunion picnic, begun in 1978, serves as a reminder of the community once built and then tossed to the winds. In the words of the former residents, "The city may be gone, but the memories live on."

No history is ever complete in its telling because the human experience is richly complex. It is hoped that this book will prompt the gathering and presenting of even more stories that comprise the history of Russell City.

One

ESTABLISHMENTS AND
MOVEMENTS

Prior to First Contact, an abundant ecological system provided for a thriving Ohlone culture near the bay. Natural resources—mussels, abalone, clams, salmon, sturgeon, and lamprey, as well as waterfowl, deer and elk, possum, ground squirrels, and rabbits—were common to the region. A verdant landscape provided for ample edible plants, including the oak trees that were native to the region, whose acorns were a mainstay for most California Indian diets. Woven reed canoes were used by the Ohlones to navigate the bay. The Yrgin Ohlones were the people who developed villages and resided in the area that came to be known, over the centuries, by several names: Russell's, Russell District, Little Copenhagen, Russell City, and Hayward. (Courtesy of the Bancroft Library, University of California, Berkeley; illustration by Ludvik Choris.)

When Spanish colonialists arrived in the region in 1769, they were accompanied by Franciscan priests intent on proselytizing the Ohlone people. This drawing was created sometime during the first decade of the 1800s, when the predominance of Ohlones had been moved—some through coercion and others willingly—to Mission San José. These six men with elaborately painted and tattooed bodies, wearing costumes and headdresses, participate in a ritual dance. This illustration by Georg Heinrich von Langsdorff is thought to be the earliest known view of Ohlone Indians in native clothing at the mission. (Courtesy of the Bancroft Library, University of California, Berkeley.)

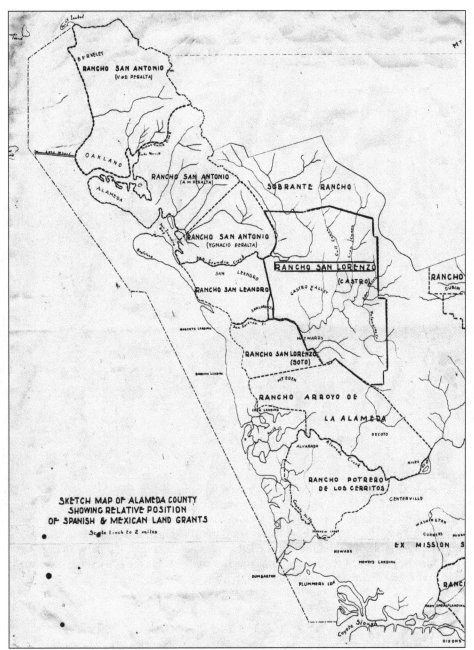

SKETCH MAP OF ALAMEDA COUNTY
SHOWING RELATIVE POSITION
OF SPANISH & MEXICAN LAND GRANTS
Scale 1 inch to 2 miles

The Treaty of Guadalupe Hidalgo guaranteed property rights to the Californios who lived in the region annexed to the United States in 1848. Congressional legislation in the form of the Federal Land Law of 1851 required that those who held deeds of title derived from Spanish or Mexican land grants appear before the U.S. Land Commission and prove the validity of their claims to the property. The average case remained in litigation for about 17 years. Over three fourths of the claims or 588 land grants throughout the state, totaling 8,850,143 acres, were adjudicated in favor of the claimants. Francisco Soto was forced to defend Rancho San Lorenzo before the land commission. He died before the dispute was resolved, but his wife, Barbara Castro de Soto, prevailed in her assertion of the family's claim to the land.

13

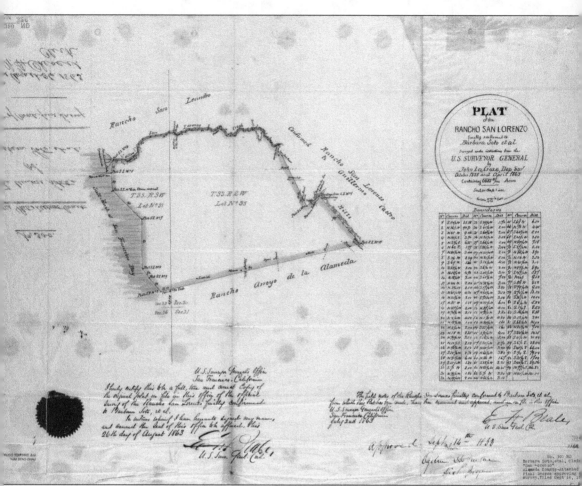

This is the official plat of the Rancho San Lorenzo. It confirmed ownership to Barbara Castro de Soto and her family. This pen-and-ink and watercolor on tracing cloth plat indicates drainage, survey markers, boundaries, township and section lines, adjoining ranchos, and other important markers. It also includes a table of boundaries and surveyor general's certifications and seal noted on the right-hand side. The shading on the left-hand side of the plat indicates the bay, and the middle to lower portion of the rancho that touches the bay became Russell City. (Courtesy of the Bancroft Library, University of California, Berkeley.)

Joel Russell was born in Maine in the year 1822. He attended the Bethel Academy in Medford, Massachusetts. At the age of 27, he took passage on the *Henry Ware* and traveled to San Francisco by way of Cape Horn. Between 1850 and 1851, he spent time farming in Stockton, a venture that proved unsuccessful for him. Unable to master the craft, Russell left for San Francisco. In 1853, he traveled to the East Bay and squatted on land owned by Barbara Castro de Soto and her family. By 1856, Russell had reached an agreement with Soto to purchase a portion of Rancho San Lorenzo that was located about 1.5 miles east of the bay.

In 1856, Joel Russell married Carrie Bartlett, who, like Russell, was a native of Maine who migrated to California. She taught Latin at Mt. Eden School. They raised three children: Maud, Thomas, and Frederick. They had a fourth child, Laura, who died at the age of two. Joel Russell was a successful judge, political activist, and real estate developer. Initially, he was active in the Republican Party and a staunch abolitionist. Later he joined the Prohibitionist Party, possibly because of the involvement of his wife, Carrie Bartlett Russell, in the Women's Christian Temperance Union. Joel Russell was elected justice of the peace for Eden Township in 1854. He was an unsuccessful candidate for California governor in 1866 as a Prohibition Party candidate. His real property holdings included the bayside land as well as significant portions of downtown Hayward, including the property that would one day become Hayward Union High School. He is shown here with daughter Maud Falkner Russell (left) and wife, Carrie Bartlett Russell (center). (Courtesy of Barbara Russell.)

Maud Falkner Russell was a young woman of 29 when she died of a consumptive ailment, according to Barbara Russell, the great-great granddaughter of Joel and Carrie. Maud was characterized in family lore as a young woman who placed importance on all manners of appearance in garb and in geniality. (Courtesy of Barbara Russell.)

On the High Seas   Feb 26 '86

NIHILITY

When roses bloom and violets are plenty
And pansies lift in innocence their faces glad
About the tomb of hopes at four and twenty
Linger my tho'ts in retrospection sad.

Ah! hopes of mine that built in ambition's granite
    And in designs symmetrical and grand
T'were vain to list for song as in the olden fashion.

There bursts no paen now from halls that once were vocal
    The shock of circumstance ye could not stand
Sweet hopes and fair, alas but for endurance fragile.

    Linger not long 'mid shades of four and twenty;
Life's days to come are filled with duties yet;
    Morn's roses bloom and violets are plenty
And pansies lift dew-radiant their faces wet.

                        Maud F. Russell

(This was written on the way back from Tahaiti less
    than two months before she died, April 20)

She would have reached the age of 29 June 14, 1886.

Maud had been sent to Tahiti to recover, but the travel did not benefit her condition. This poem written by her en route home is prefaced: "On the high seas Feb 26 '86." The poem has an endnote by an unnamed writer, who said, "This was written on the way back from Tahaiti [sic] less than two months before she died, April 20. She would have reached the age of 29 June 14, 1886." The content of the poem titled "Nihility" indicates that perhaps Maud was reflecting on a more joyful time of her short life. (Courtesy of Barbara Russell.)

From left to right are Lloyd Smalley, Lelia Mildred, Maud Muriel, and Thomas Bartlett Jr. who were the children of Thomas Bartlett Sr. and Lelia May Smalley Russell. Thomas Sr. acquired the downtown holdings of the family after the death of his parents, Joel and Carrie. His brother, Frederick, would acquire the bayside property later known as Russell City. (Courtesy of Barbara Russell.)

Although separated by geography, the children of Thomas Bartlett Sr. and Lelia Smalley Russell occasionally found time to reunite. They are in the backyard of their parents' home, located on land that is now the center of the intersection at Russell Way and Second Street. From left to right are (first row) Lelia Mildred and Thomas Bartlett Jr.; (second row) Lloyd Smalley and Maud Muriel. Maud Muriel, named for her aunt, became a Marxist as the result of conditions she saw in the provinces of China while working with the YWCA in their various missions during the 1920s and 1930s. As a result of her beliefs and affiliations, Maud was called before the U.S. House of Representatives Committee on Un-American Activities in 1963. A lesbian, she lived her later years in New York City, where she died and is buried. (Courtesy of Jan Chandler Hunter.)

Thanksgiving Day in the 1940s found the Russell family celebrating at their home in downtown Hayward. From left to right are Eleanor Russell Chandler, George Smalley, Maud Muriel Russell, Lelia Smalley Russell, Barbara Russell, and Thomas Bartlett Russell Jr. Eleanor and Barbara are the daughters of Thomas Bartlett Jr. (Courtesy of Jan Chandler Hunter.)

Joel Russell subdivided his land and began to embark on his most successful of enterprises: real estate development. He sold lots to newly arrived immigrant families: Nielsen, Hansen, Pelagore, Michelsen, Pestdorf, Madsen, Tucksen, and Christensen, among others. Because of the large numbers of Danish immigrants like this family who lived in the area, people from Hayward referred to the collection of families as "Little Copenhagen." They grew hay, wheat, grain, and corn, as well as peas and beans. Cherry, pear, and apricot trees were plentiful, along with a few currant orchards. Most of the men were trained carpenters and initially found jobs building homes or working in the nearby salt ponds in order to raise money for the purchase of their own farmlands. (Courtesy of Linda Mateos Milistefr.)

Neils Peter (N. P.) Nielsen emigrated from the village of Velling, Denmark, in 1885. Soon after his arrival in the area, he bought 10 acres of land from Joel Russell. The proximity of the bay must have appealed to those who were accustomed to living so close to open water. The diversity of the bay wildlife sustained those who lived in the area well into the early 20th century. N. P. appears here to have returned from hunting local waterfowl, which were said to be in great abundance. (Courtesy of Muriel Manter Knickerbocker.)

N. P. Nielsen built his family a stately home for $2,500. It contained a full basement, and its porches and gables were crafted in the highly embellished Victorian style of the time. The home was located on an unnamed country road that eventually became Russell Road and then West Winton Avenue. Vivian Nygren Ross-Brown describes farms of the area as laid out in a "typical Scandinavian format . . . the barn and grain field and cows in one area . . . vegetable garden in another . . . fruit trees had their space (apricot, pear, crabapple, peach, and fig) . . . flower gardens went around the house . . . and beautiful shade trees scattered here and there." (Courtesy of Muriel Manter Knickerbocker.)

The Hansen home was located in the enclave of Danes, whose population was small but growing to include German, Swiss, and Dutch immigrant families. Many of the Danish families came from the Als area of Denmark, located in the region near the German border. The outbreak of World War I caused for some interesting moments of national pride. Muriel Manter Knickerbocker recalls her mother's upset many years after the end of that war because one of the German families painted their windmill in the colors of the German flag. That home still stands on the corner of West Winton and Corsair Streets.

Carpentry was a skill that many brought with them from their homelands, and the Christiansen family was no different in that regard. The heritage of those talents was continued well into the 20th century when a member of the Christiansen family assisted in the construction of the 1939 Golden Gate International Exposition on Treasure Island. The back of this postcard reads, "My old home about 1895. Mr. and Mrs. Henningsen and Ma and Pa.—Lulu."

The Madsen home was built on a lane that intersected Russell Road right before it ended on the western shore. Because of the farm's proximity to the bay, the family was able to construct salt ponds in the back of the home in addition to having vegetable crops and an orchard. Muriel Manter Knickerbocker recalls that the adults from the various Danish families of Russell played parlor games from their homeland and that Skærvindsel, a short deck card game, was an especially popular diversion when the families gathered at the Madsen home.

This Carlsen family home was bequeathed to Anine Carlsen Horat, the wife of Fred Horat. She lived there until 1957. The home was located at 8611 Russell Road. (Courtesy of Loretta Horat Machado.)

23

After the Michelsen family had saved sufficient funds, they built this home, their second. It was located on Russell Road at the intersection of Clawiter Road. Their daughter married N. P. Nielsen, who lived nearby. During 1942, the home and land were acquired from the family in order to accommodate military operations during World War II. The landing field was called the Russell City Army Air Field. Today the Hayward Air National Guard is stationed on that property. (Courtesy of Muriel Manter Knickerbocker.)

This was originally home to the Nielsen family, and when their daughter Anna married Harold Nygren, the young couple created an extended family by residing with the Nielsens. Various members of the Nygren-Nielsen families, seen here, lived together in this residence from the 1880s to the 1970s. The section of the home where the brick chimney is located is the original structure; the other portions were added in subsequent years. According to Vivian Nygren Ross-Brown, granddaughter of the descendants seen here, a golden brown Jersey was one of two cows, the other a black and white Holstein, which were perennial breeds owned by the family. (Courtesy of Karen Verili.)

After Joel and Carrie Russell died, the estate went to their sons, Thomas and Frederick. Thomas acquired the land located in downtown Hayward. Frederick became the owner of "the ranch," the family name for the property by the bay. Frederick is shown here with his wife, Nellie, under a portrait of his aunt, Maud Falkner Russell. (Courtesy of Linda Mateos Milistefr.)

RUSSELL CITY

The New City on San Francisco Bay

AND

The Best Investment in California To-Day

Lots
$200
and up

Ten per cent down and $5.00 per month

No Interest
No Taxes

Perfect Climate

One Hour from San Francisco or Twenty-five Minutes from Oakland to

Russell City

This is the biggest suburban lot proposition on the market. Choice building lots for sale. 1351 sold to date. Lots are going rapidly. Send coupon on opposite page for free ticket.

EAST SHORE & SUBURBAN REALTY COMPANY

1015 Broadway, Oakland, Cal.   2195 Bush St., San Francisco, Cal.

Frederick Russell worked with a real estate consortium to develop the bayside property into an upscale suburban enclave. They named the development Russell City after Frederick's father and held out the promise of a "perfect climate" and rapid commute times to San Francisco and Oakland. Lots sold for $200 and up. They mistakenly believed that after the 1906 quake the residents of San Francisco would flee the city for their community. Most San Franciscans remained in their beloved city by the bay, and those who departed left for burgeoning destinations like Oakland and San José.

Russell City, as seen here in a 1907 conceptual drawing, was subdivided into rectangular parcels. A grand avenue complete with palm trees and a parkway was planned to run down the center of this imagined bayside city. The dream was never realized, however. Infrastructure such as sewer, electrical and gas utilities, curbs, and gutters were never brought to the community. The low-lying water table, as well as the lack of utilities and amenities necessary to habitability, made for a shaky foundation to begin such a project. Added to these elements were the cycle of early- to mid-20th-century recessions in the economy and the Great Depression, which contributed to the failure of the housing development.

Two

MIGRANTS AND
IMMIGRANTS

Beginning with the Yrgin Ohlones, people collected salt from the briny bay waters in what became one of the enduring bayside enterprises. Channels and sloughs crossed the natural tidal marshlands. The Yrgins harvested salt by inserting reeds into the shoreline waters, and as the natural evaporation occurred, it resulted in a residue of salt on the reed for consumption. The Spanish, Mexicans, and Californios required large quantities of salt for the tanning of hides and preservation of beef, and they greatly expanded the processes. Their collection ponds were called *salinas*. The advent of the Gold Rush brought thousands from around the world to Northern California. Basic foods became precious commodities, including salt, which sometimes commanded as much as $50 an ounce. Small cabins built on pilings dotted the ponds and served as refuge from inclement weather. Cabins similar to those seen in this photograph can be seen deteriorating along the still productive salt ponds in nearby Newark.

This the original Michelsen home, built near the bay in the Russell District. There is a wind-driven screw pump to the left of the home. Its use in the salt ponds was to transfer brine from one pond to another as part of the production process. The pump is called an Archimedes screw, named for the ancient Greek philosopher and inventor. (Courtesy of Muriel Manter Knickerbocker.)

This 1882 illustration of the Russell District shows several of the wind-powered Archimedes screws in the background. There are mounds of salt and pond workers in the area above the barns and homes. In the center road comes a driver with an empty horse-driven wagon en route to be filled with salt for delivery. This landing was the bay access for sailing vessels coming to the Russell District. (Courtesy of Linda Mateos Milistefr.)

The *Hayward* was a sailing scow seen anchored here at the landing located in the Russell District. The cargo is likely to have been salt and other products from Russell headed for San Francisco. A scow is a flat-bottomed boat typically used to haul freight. Scows were useful for traveling the bay because they could navigate shallow waters and be beached for loading and unloading. Further, their angular shape made them easier to construct than bowed vessels.

A steamer seen here carrying salt to its intended destination of San Francisco was one of numerous small water vessels that crossed the bay, transporting cargo and passengers. As has been noted, the locations for loading and unloading goods and people were numerous and frequently changed names depending on ownership and location. (Courtesy of Muriel Manter Knickerbocker.)

These workers are at the Mt. Eden location of the National Salt Company ponds. The workers wore high rubber boots necessary for sloshing about in the briny water of the ponds. At one time, there were 17 salt production companies in the immediate area that produced 17,000 tons of salt per year. In 1913, these ponds were sold to the Oliver family. (Courtesy of Muriel Manter Knickerbocker.)

Hans Michelsen, a cousin to the family that resided in Russell, is at the helm of this sailboat on a nearby slough behind the family home. Notice the tranquility of the water as the boat breaks its surface, as well as the large mounds of salt in the background. (Courtesy of Muriel Manter Knickerbocker.)

Climbing to the top of a salt mound is not as romantic as going to the top of Yosemite's Half Dome. Although not as steep, the ascent is not as easy as one might imagine, especially when wearing a woolen suit and long dresses. The adjacent salt ponds were important sources of employment and occasional diversion. (Courtesy of Linda Mateos Milistefr.)

Andrew Johnson was an immigrant who had purchased land from Joel Russell and initially worked as a barge operator. Johnson became a station agent for the Southern Pacific Coast Railroad when the company built a stop in Russell City. The stop was a simple platform, which in 1887, Johnson upgraded to a covered structure as seen here. He served as the agent until his retirement in 1921. The station is noted in a 1929 schedule of trains and was part of the smaller local system that traveled between the Fruitvale District in Oakland and Santa Clara. Mt. Eden was the other stop in this area. For those traveling to San Francisco or San José, a transfer was required on one of the other lines.

Andrew Johnson was also the proprietor of the single store in town, whose inventory he determined and conveyed via the ferry he owned and the train station he staffed. The store contained a community hall at the rear where celebrations where held. Although Russell City was not officially incorporated as a city, Johnson was named "mayor" of the town. While records are inconclusive as to how this honorific title came about, possibly it resulted from his authority as one who controlled the transportation and information hubs of the town. His home can be seen in the background, and it served as the residence to several generations of Johnsons.

HAYWARD PLANT 1897

An abundance of fresh produce grown in the Hayward area brought new businesses that purchased and processed the bounty of the many orchards and fields. In 1895, the Hunt brothers relocated their cannery to Hayward. The plant processed tons of produce grown locally and was an important source of employment for people living in the area, including the residents of Russell City. Carmen Liranzo Mateos recalled, "We all had our own gardens, our own chickens, beef cattle, rabbits, and milk cows." In 1950, the *Hayward Daily Review* reported that April 1 was the official start of the asparagus season, followed by cherry and apricot season in June, tomato season in mid-July, and that Hunt's Cannery maintains 500 workers in the off-season.

Fred Gavello's maternal grandfather, Giovanni Pertino, came from Albisola, Italy, in 1912, leaving his wife and daughter behind until he could work and raise the money to bring them to the United States. In 1920, he bought a 20-acre farm in Russell City and brought his wife, Clara, and daughter Pierina over. Pierina became Fred's mother. The Pertino farm was located on Grant Street, southeast of Russell Road. They raised vegetables, including beans, peas, garlic, and cauliflower. Livestock included cows, horses, pigs, sheep, goats, chickens, and ducks. Clara and Giovanni Pertino are standing amid their farm with an unidentified child and one of the field hands in the background. (Courtesy of Fred Gavello.)

This 1934 photograph shows, from left to right, Giovanni Pertino, holding baby Pierina, sitting next to three neighbors: Claude "Jack" Jackson, Barney Matousek, and Claudine Jackson Matousek. Fred Gavello Sr. and his mother, Clara Pertino Gavello, sit next to them. The Camenzind Dairy is in the background of this field. (Courtesy of Fred Gavello.)

In the year 1925, the six Horat brothers moved from Switzerland to Russell City: Fred, Tobias, Albert, Karolina (center), Pete, Damion, and Joseph. Karolina, the matriarch, seen here visiting her sons, returned to live in Switzerland with the only sister in the family. The Horats established a successful dairy at the western edge of Russell near the Santucci Hog Farm. It is said that when Fred and Albert delivered milk, they yodeled their arrival. (Courtesy of Loretta Horat Machado.)

Joseph Horat, pictured here in 1980 with his dog, lived on the dairy until 1986. He was, when he moved, the oldest and longest living person, in Russell City. (Courtesy of Linda Mateos Milistefr.)

In 1936, a cousin of Earl Wallis showed him a photograph of his sweetheart back in Oklahoma. Earl asked about the girl standing next to her and was told that she was the sweetheart's cousin Ruth. On the spot, Earl declared, "That's the girl for me. One day I'll marry that girl." He bean a correspondence with Ruth, and a year later in 1937, she came to California to visit an aunt in Visalia. Fred drove out to the valley to meet her. A week after meeting, Earl and Ruth drove to Reno, where they were married. Their marriage lasted more than 60 years and only ended when Earl passed away in 2004. Their first home as a couple was located on Russell Road; they paid rent of $7 a month. (Courtesy of Ruth Wallis.)

The Cota family moved to Russell City in 1938 from Brawley, California, in the Imperial Valley; prior to that, the family had lived in Calexico. Joe Cota, who was a child when the family moved to Russell, recalls that the home into which they moved was more shack than home. Joe slept in a tent during the time that the family was rehabilitating the home for themselves. In spite of the difficult circumstances, Magdalena Cota Leon, seen here, always maintained a garden and was proud of her green thumb. (Courtesy of Joe Cota.)

Gardens were common elements in the yards of Russell City homes. Neighbors traded the bounty of their fruit orchards and vegetable gardens with one another. This is the Figueroa family garden with Faustino Jr., Faustino Sr., and James taking a break from their yard work. (Courtesy of James and Priscilla Figueroa.)

In 1947, Fred and Joseph Gavello received this brown Swiss calf from the Horat family as payment for the removal of sugar beet tops from the fields owned by the Liranzo family. The Horats used the beet tops as feed for their herd of dairy cows. The Gavello boys were given the calf on condition that should they ever decide not to keep it they would return the cow to the Horats. The calf grew up quite accustomed to human contact and as a result was more a member of the Gavello family than a working dairy cow. Mt. Eden is seen in the background of this photograph. (Courtesy of Fred Gavello.)

Regardless of the time in its history, life was demanding for the residents of Russell City. Rural existence required people young and old to work continuously in the farm or around the home. Here one of the elder Nielsens of the Nygren-Nielsen family is pitching hay behind the barn. (Courtesy of Karen Verili.)

Giovanni Pertino is shown with a horse working his vegetable farm in the late 1920s. Farm animals were critical to the success of the different agricultural enterprise in the community. As a result, the livestock were treated well and were integral working four-legged members of the family. (Courtesy of Fred Gavello.)

Some farming enterprises were less advanced in their ability to apply modern methods to their production. Eventually the use of the gas-powered equipment became pervasive in the small community, but not everyone could afford such costly machinery.

This early hay bailer was used by the Horat Dairy. The Horat Dairy was located at the end of Russell Road by the bay. There were two other dairies in Russell City: Holdener and Camenzind. The Holdener Dairy was located north of Russell Road behind the library. The Camenzind Dairy was south of Russell Road. (Courtesy of Loretta Horat Machado.)

The Horat Dairy was still prosperous 25 years after its start by the six founding Swiss brothers. Loretta Horat (left) and her friend Lois Tavis (right) are pictured taking a time out from work in 1953. (Courtesy of Loretta Horat Machado.)

Carl Liranzo was fascinated by heavy machinery from the time he was a little boy. His happy face seen here as he readies his International Harvester is apparent. Carl was elated when in 1960 for $25 he was able to purchase and renovate a 1912 fire truck, a "Little Giant" model. His parents migrated from Spain to Russell City. They lived on a 20-acre farm whose boundaries were Lincoln and Monroe Streets. The children—Carl, Mary, and Carmen—were all born in Russell City. (Courtesy of Linda Mateos Milistefr.)

In keeping with the agrarian roots of the area, the various local school districts maintained active agricultural education programs for students. This hay baler was one of the pieces of equipment on which students were trained in the 1950s and 1960s. The teaching farm for the Hayward area was located in Russell City and later, after its demolition, was moved to the Mt. Eden area.

The Camenzind family owned the largest of the Russell City dairies, seen here in an aerial shot. It is easy to observe the large quantity of land devoted to the thriving business. Louis Camenzind immigrated to Russell City from Switzerland in 1903. He and his wife, Mary, raised six daughters and two sons. One of the daughters, Martha, recalled, "It was a lot of hard work—milking cows, cutting hay, and irrigating—, but we all had a good time."

Located at the end of Russell Road, next to the Horat Dairy, Santucci Hog Farm, also known as the Russell City Hog Farm, is best known for the malodorous perfume it sent into the air of the community. In spite of the evil smell of the hogs, children of the area, now grown into elders, recall with glee the fun they had riding the hogs and the horror of their mothers when they returned home reeking from their play. (Courtesy of Barber Joe.)

From left to right are Johnny and Mary Garcia, Julio Santucci, and Carmen Liranzo, who are enjoying a lighthearted moment before Santucci left for service in World War II. Regrettably, Santucci would die in the war. (Courtesy of Linda Mateos Milistefr.)

One of four grocery stories in Russell City, James's Store located on Washington Street contained an eclectic array of goods ranging from canned goods to aspirin, candy and other treats, cigarettes, and alcoholic beverages. Older students, from left to right center, Zenobia Kimball, Dorothy Trotter, and Vincent Gimeno shop for treats after school. (Courtesy of William Mette.)

Charles (seated, center) and Pauline Tourchette (standing) identified themselves as "Louisiana-French." They had nine children. The five seen here are, from left to right, Elizabeth, Joe, Barbara, Edolie, and Eli. The Tourchettes were owners of a gas station and small grocery store located at the intersection of Russell Road and the railroad tracks. The family home sat atop the store. The entire building burned down in 1952, killing the patriarch Charles and leaving Pauline to raise nine children herself. (Courtesy of Connie Anderson.)

The Reynolds family home (left) and auto repair (right) were located on Monroe Street. Because so many young men in the community were proud car owners, the Reynolds's Garage was a popular destination for them after school and on weekends. (Courtesy of Loretta Horat Machado.)

The Hayward Rug Works was a plant that hired young people in the community for small jobs. It was located on Russell Road near the Nygren-Nielsen home, across from the school.

At one point, the Hayward Rug Works expanded to include upholstery cleaning and repair. It was a popular business in the area because it provided pickup and delivery services.

At the end of Russell Road was a garbage dump. The decision to create and maintain such a high toxin-generating business was probably because the dairy and hog farm were already in existence in that area of Russell City. The combination of all three businesses contributed mightily to the toxic waste that ran into the bay, leeched into the soil, and befouled the air.

This rural landscape of homes, backyards, and garages provides some indication of the condition in which people lived in portions of the community. (Courtesy of William Mette.)

This was the Reynolds home, which was located next to their auto repair, Reynolds's Garage. Although the entirety of the landscape is unpaved, the family has made attempts at beautification through the use of decorative plantings around the perimeter of the home. (Courtesy of Loretta Horat Machado.)

This is the intersection of Russell Road, now West Winton Avenue, and Hesperian Boulevard. Note that the number of vehicles traveling on the road and the homes nearby did not impress upon public officials to provide basics such as asphalt paving, curbs and gutters, or traffic lights to the community.

By contrast, this photograph of downtown Hayward at the intersection of B Street and Foothill Boulevard indicates the disparity of treatment in the two adjacent communities. Although there appears to be several collisions in the making, there are traffic signals and crosswalks to guide the flow of vehicles and pedestrians.

This is the appearance of Russell Road when the rain came. The potholes and ruts were a constant threat to the maintenance of an automobile's wheel alignment.

The Southern Pacific Railroad line is still active today through this portion of Hayward. When Russell City was in existence, the children were warned of the dangers of the tracks. What the community could not control was the impaired judgment of those who left the various bars in the area and attempted to unsafely travel across the tracks to beat the train. This photograph was shot by Thomas Eddens, who was at the time, a high school student taking pictures for a class project. (Courtesy of Mildred Jean Hill-Eddens.)

Knee-Hi, a dog mascot, is assisting this officer in a 1954 traffic stop on Russell Road. Rosie Rivers (second from left) and Robert Trotter (fourth from left) are continuing on to school with their friends. (Courtesy of William Mette.)

Even the school was not exempt from the lack of consideration by public officials. A note from Russell Public School principal Wilda Mette written in January 1950 and attached to this photograph reads, "When it rains the driveway becomes a mud slough for these children at Russell." (Courtesy of William Mette.)

Three

LEARNING INSTITUTIONS

Prior to the establishment of the Russell Public School in 1897, children attended Mt. Eden School. N. P. Nielsen, Jens Hansen, Peter Mathiesen, Andrew Johnson, and others living in the Russell area consulted with county authorities and local residents about the need for a school. The first classes were held in September 1897 with 30 pupils and one teacher in charge of teaching all grade levels. When this photograph was taken in 1916, there was still but one teacher.

This 1911 portrait includes all of the students enrolled in the school at the time. As noted by their surnames, the students reflect the continued presence of Danish, Swedish, German, and Swiss families in the area. Pictured are, from left to right, (first row) Ethel Nissen, Agnes Nielsen, Mildred Chistensen, Annie Carlsen, and Tillie McCoy; (second row) Elsie/Thelma Bohnet, Rebecca Christensen, Amy Tacker, and Amos Alsing; (third row) Julius Anderson, Harry Christensen, and Axel Anderson; (fourth row) Florence Pestdorf, Mary Asmussen, Cora Anderson, Christine Nielsen, and Helen Russell; (fifth row) Metha Christensen, Charlie Nissen, Hazel Alsing, Perry Hansen, Katy Hansen, Henry Kahlke, and Helga Nielsen. Helga Nielsen became a teacher at Hayward Union High School, where she worked for 42 years. (Courtesy of Linda Mateos Milistefr.)

By the 1920s, the surrounding population had grown considerably, as mirrored in the quantity of students now attending the school. Reflected, too, in the faces of the students was the expanding cultural diversity of the region. Spanish, Japanese, and Italian families such as Liranzo, Kawahara, and Pertino were establishing their homes and farms in Russell City. (Courtesy of Linda Mateos Milistefr.)

Margaret Feldman (left) shared teaching responsibilities with May Holzman (right). At one time, there were eight grade levels and each of these teachers taught a single class that combined four grade levels. Holzman was, in addition to being a teacher, the school principal. (Courtesy of Linda Mateos Milistefr.)

Taken during the 1930s, this Russell Public School photograph indicates the growth in population and expansion of the cultural diversity in the town. Still present in the community were the Danish, German, Swiss, Spanish, Japanese, and Italian families, now joined by Mexican, Puerto Rican, Filipino, and African American families. Shown here are, from left to right, (first row) Alfred Bucol, Ernest ?, Junior ?, John Brookshier, Tony ?, Jimmy Perry, Sidney Christensen, Geopesto Bucol, three unidentified, Ralph Garcia, unidentified, Andrew ?, two unidentified, Tony Bucol, unidentified, ? Paqua, unidentified, Jimmy Bucol, George ?, and one unidentified; (second row) Gene Rollier, "Baby" Renie, Helen ?, unidentified, Victoria ?, Julia ?, Minnie ?, Dorothy ?,

Alvera ?, Deloris ?, Marion ?, Anna ?, Ethel ?, Pauline May Gotten, Rosie ?, five unidentified, Bonnie ?, unidentified, Phyllis ?, Lola ?, and three unidentified; (third row) ? Stern, ? Feldman, Rodney Christensen, Charles Madsen, May ?, Lupe ?, Betty ?, Elizabeth ?, Mary Pacheco, Mary Perry, Frank Perry, Barbara Manter, Eileen Brookshier, Chio ?, Pete Ybarra, ? Perino, Vincent ?, John Ybarra, Albert ?, Jean Carrine, Paul Solis, two unidentified, Harry ?, David ?, and Chris Perry; (fourth row) ? Holzman, Mary Solis, Jennie ?, Mildred Camenzind, Carmen Liranzo, Ruth Rollins, Lila Torres, Renie Garcia, Muriel Manter, John Madsen, John ?, Ruben ?, James Jacks, Louie ?, Melvin Lacy, Crispen ?, Jessie ?, Enrico ?, Peter ?, Trinidad ?, Julius ?, and Earl ?. (Courtesy of Muriel Manter Knickerbocker.)

Graduation ceremonies were formal occasions at Russell Public School. Each student who completed eighth-grade studies during the 1930s received a pin indicating their year of graduation. This 1938 pin belonged to Carmen Liranzo. Carmen concluded her formal studies with this graduation. She went on to become the owner of a small grocery at the age of 16 and then the proprietor of numerous business concerns, including the Mt. Eden Mushroom Farm. She exhibited a sharp business mind, which, coupled with her ability for frank observation, made for a successful entrepreneur. Carmen married Albert Mateos, a local boy, and together they raised their daughters, Linda and Pearl, in nearby Mt. Eden. (Courtesy of Kim Milistefr Finn.)

The Nygren daughters, from left to right, Violet, Vivian, and Verna stand on the porch of their grandmother Karen Nielsen, whose front rooms became the Russell Library. Hours are seen posted on the front door. A history of the libraries of Alameda County was created in 1939 as part of a WPA project. The story of each existing library was told with a watercolor painting and handmade calligraphy. This is what that history said about the Russell Library: "Russell may have dreamed of being a city some day, but it is still only a country cross-roads, in a Danish community where the farmers are well educated, with high ideals, and have provided comfortable homes for their families. Here, right across from the school, stands a sizable home whose owner set about to build another small house beside his own, so Russell branch, established August 1917, was the first branch library to have at the beginning a home built especially to house it. Well furnished inside and out, it presents a very attractive appearance with its pretty garden, and a brick walk leading to the door. Book cases were built in, and the farmer's wife receives the books and magazines, checking them in and out, as the neighbor's come and go." (Courtesy of Karen Verili.)

From left to right, Anna Nielsen Nygren, holding daughters Violet and Vivian, sits on the front porch of her home that was built next to the smaller home, whose front rooms became the library. Anna staffed the library when it first opened in 1917. According to the historical records maintained by the Alameda County Library, in 1923, "Anna Nielsen Nygren had a small building erected on the lot next door to her mother's home for the use of the library. This was the first library erected for the use of a county library branch." (Courtesy of Karen Verili.)

In August 1950, Anna Nielsen Nygren's husband, Harold Nygren, enlarged the Russell Library. The space grew from 256 to 736 square feet. Space for more books was necessary, as the population of the community was continuing to grow and demands for service were high. Russell Public School teacher Gertrude Knowles (left) and principal Wilda Mette (right) post a notice announcing a community meeting regarding civil safety matters; the information is written in English and Spanish.

Anna Nielsen Nygren was much loved by students at the Russell Public School that was located across the street. She nourished their minds with sound reading recommendations and provided sustenance for the tummy with after-school cookies and milk. Anna Nielsen Nygren continued her service as the librarian for the Russell Library until she retired in 1960. Her salary at the time of retirement was $395 a month. From left to right, Lanny Ross, Lillian Brown, Helen Versalles, and Joe Tolefree enjoy a moment with their favorite educator. (Courtesy of Karen Verili.)

This majestic Carnegie Library was located on the northeast corner of B Street and First Street (now Foothill Boulevard). The library was torn down when Foothill was widened during the 1950s. Thomas Bartlett Sr. and his son, Thomas Bartlett Jr., are in the carriage surveying the little damage incurred in the downtown as a result of the 1906 earthquake. Compared to the modest home library in Russell City, this was a magnificent public asset for Hayward.

The original school was razed to make way for this 1940 modern school facility. Between the years 1946 and 1955, pupil enrollment grew from 230 to 400 students. There were so many students that space limitations required the school to operate on double sessions between 1946 and 1950. Officials reported, "By 1955 nine more classrooms were constructed, facilities provided for special education classes, playground equipment was installed, and the school site was graded and paved." When the school was closed in 1957, longtime teacher and principal Wilda Mette retired.

It might have been intimidating for students who graduated from Russell Public School to continue on to Hayward Union High School, located 5 miles away in downtown Hayward. The expansive three-story high school with its classical Greek Ionic architectural elements was considered one of the most elegant schools in the nation. Before its construction, students from the area who wanted to continue their education by going to high school had to travel to Oakland High School for their studies. The land on which the high school was built belonged to Joel Russell, who sold it to the trustees after a 1911 bond measure, which raised funds to construct the school, passed. This election was notable for the fact that it was the first time Hayward women were permitted suffrage, as earlier that year California men had passed a measure expanding the right to vote to women.

Faculty at the Russell Public School in 1956 included, from left to right, (first row) Cleveland Livingston, Gertrude Knowles, Dorothy Scott, Mary Micheo, Jean Sorenson, Vivian Abbott, Eva White, and Roy Hanson; (second row) Ruth Halverson, Anne McWhinney, Ruth Peterson, Elsie Baker, Christine Manter, Nell Hicks, Bob Keropian, and school principal Wilda Mette.

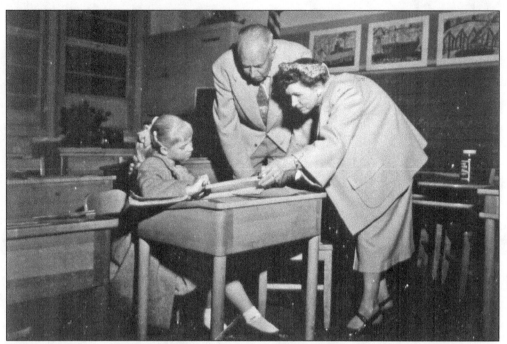

This photograph, taken shortly before Anna Nielsen Nygren's retirement as librarian, shows her with her husband, Harold Nygren, who was clerk for the Russell Public School Board. The student at the desk is La Voy Anderson.

It is not an exaggeration to say that students enjoyed happy and healthy learning relationships with the educators at the Russell Public School. Wayne Johnigan (left) and Arthur Charles "AC" Tolefree (right) were featured with principal Wilda Mette in this photograph for a "Smile of the Week" competition held by the local newspaper, the *Hayward Daily Review*.

Celebrations were common in the school for students and teachers alike. This surprise party for homemaking teacher Dorothy Scott took place in 1949 and included, standing from left to right, school principal Wilda Mette, Dorothy Scott, and Artie Johnigan, along with Sally Hernandez and Catalina Ramirez (both in front of Dorothy Scott). (Courtesy of William Mette.)

May Holzman was principal at Russell Public School from 1928 through World War II. She was feted in a 1980 gala celebration at Willow Park Country Club, where more than 300 of her former Russell Public School students attended. (Courtesy of Linda Mateos Milistefr.)

Antone Johnson, custodian for the Russell Public School, was a descendant of Andrew Johnson and lived in the home that Andrew had built on Russell Road in the 1800s. Antone is pictured here at his retirement party. Muriel Manter Knickerbocker recalled that on cold days, Antone Johnson arrived early to the school and started a "roaring five in the large potbellied stove" to keep students warm. (Courtesy of Linda Mateos Milistefr.)

Upon her retirement in 1961, Eva White wrote a brief summary of her 14 years of experience as a teacher at Russell Public School. She concluded her thoughts with these words: "It has been sweet to see glimpses of the joy of rewarded service in the improvement of human relations, in the ever increasing dependability and self-reliance of pupils, in the recognition received by many of the pupils for scholastic and social progress." She is seen here receiving her retirement recognition from a trustee of the Russell Public School Board.

In 1948, the Optimist Service Club sponsored the Cod Liver Oil Program. Russell Public School teacher Jean Sorenson is administering cod liver oil to her first-grade pupils. The motto of the program was, "In line for healthy bodies with a spoonful of 'internal sunshine.'" (Courtesy of William Mette.)

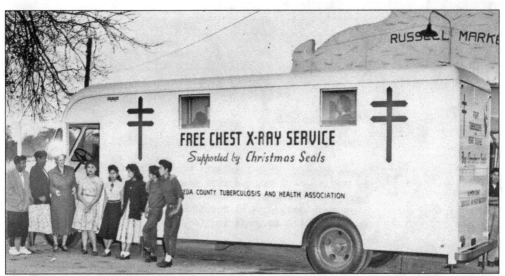

High school students from Russell City worked on shifts at this 1949 mobile health unit from 10:00 a.m. to 2:00 p.m. and from 4:00 p.m. to 7:00 p.m., assisting Alameda County Health Department doctors and nurses. The students assisted with record keeping and conducted house-to-house outreach to encourage residents to participate in the free health examinations. (Courtesy of William Mette.)

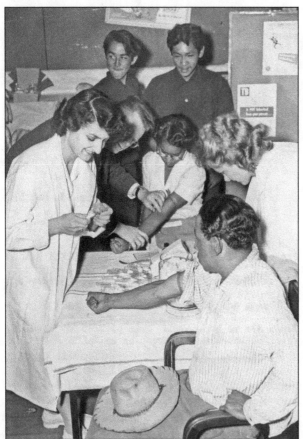

Administering blood tests to residents was part of the examination performed by, from left to right, nurse Betty Tracas, Dr. B. A. Kogan, and nurse Alice Yeagle. Hayward Union High School students who lived in Russell are in the background. These services were provided in 1949 inside the Russell Grocery, where a room sometimes served as the office. (Courtesy of William Mette.)

A traveling well baby clinic came to the community, and the visits took place in the school. This is the waiting and preparation room for the clinic. From left to right are (seated) Willie Ann Green, Carrie Green with a child, Jennie Cervantez and her girls Eva and Kelly; (standing) Artie Johnigan. (Courtesy of William Mette.)

Russell Public School teacher Eva White (third from left), student Martha Jo Bunn (center), and principal Willa Mette (not shown) traveled to Valley Forge, Pennsylvania, to receive the Freedoms Foundation Award on behalf of the school in 1950. Martha Jo Bunn was selected "Outstanding Student" by her eighth-grade peers to represent the students at the ceremony. Her "studious nature and sportsmanship at play" were cited as key reasons for her selection.

In the years 1950 and 1953, Russell Public School was one of 10 schools in the United States recognized by the Freedoms Foundation for excellence in the "programs of teaching the fundamental freedoms of American Way of Life." Teacher Eva White taught students the history and the application of Constitutional rights in their civics classes. The school vied with public and parochial schools from large cities such as Boston and Chicago in the annual awards competitions.

Important classroom teaching devices applied at the Russell Public School included the integration of reading primary sources like books, newspapers, and personal writings and discussing lessons, as well as the development of creative projects that applied the book learning and that offered students the opportunity to express their ideas in a variety of forms. Note how the students are drawing their own illustrations to indicate the various liberties provided for in the U.S. Constitution.

Field trips took students out of the classroom and into the adult world of government affairs. Here is Faye Gullat meeting with Alameda County Sheriff Howard Gleason (right) in 1953 in a county courtroom.

On this 1950 field trip to Alameda County offices in Oakland, students met Archey F. Holmes, the deputy chief supervisor with the assessor's office. He is pointing to the location of Russell City on this map—even though the year 1924 printed on it makes the map a bit out of date at the time.

Another form of learning took place by having students regularly read the local paper and critically assess its content. These students are learning about the expansion of the Hayward Municipal Airport just up the road from the school.

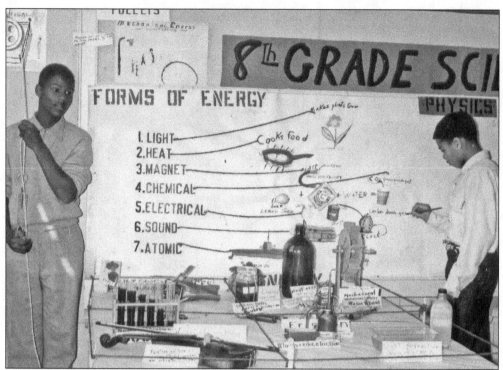

Applied science lessons offered opportunities for students to learn about the everyday applications of their studies. This particular photograph demonstrates how hands-on art-based projects gave students with a variety of learning styles chances to incorporate the knowledge into useful ideas that they could understand. Arthur Bassard (right) is noting how carbon dioxide affects the atmosphere.

Eva White, Russell Public School teacher for the eighth grade, sometimes took her classes into the fields surrounding the school. Journeys, such as this one in 1953, provided excellent hands-on opportunities for identifying and classifying botanical, biological, and ecological forms of life.

Sometimes the classroom experiences included manual labor, such as this soil preparation for planting. Pupils involved in this learning process are, from left to right, Willie Jean ?, Ezbon ?, Manual Alvarez, Wayne ?, Glenda ?, unidentified, Lora Lee, Lydia Arellano, and Annette McCoy.

This 1954 carpentry class is an example of the curricular opportunities that opened up for students after Russell Public School principal Wilda Mette secured local and federal funds for such classes. From left to right, Seferina Dominguez, Irvin Thomas, Earlene Thomas, Priscilla Barrows, Henry Gordon, Mathilda Clara, David Figueroa, and Lillian Brown beam proudly with the completion of their bookshelf project. (Courtesy of William Mette.)

During the 1940s and 1950s, the homemaking teacher supervised girls in the preparation of lunch trays to distribute to Russell Public School students. Rachel Nava (second from right) is assisting in the work. This work provided domestic and commercial culinary training to the students. (Courtesy of William Mette.)

A written recollection crafted by former teacher Eva White in 1960 recalls that the lunchroom became an opportunity to teach children dining comportment, as well as to introduce them to lessons in nutrition and health. She said, "Tasty meals and welcome companionship in the lunch room are a welcome break in a school day. Everyone knows the simple rules of table etiquette." (Courtesy of William Mette.)

Former students recall that operetta performances were fairly common at Russell Public School. Perhaps this was an abridged version of *Carmen*. The boys are wearing bullfighters' capes, and the girls have lovely mantillas and painted fans as accessories. Ishmael Arellano, Charles Gullat (second and third from left), Howard Santiago (left center), Edith Eddens (center), Ray Armanda (right center), and Janet Rackowicz (third from right) are singing in full voice for the audience in this 1955 production. (Courtesy of William Mette.)

The Russell Public School boasted a full orchestra with strings, woodwinds, brass, and percussion instruments available to students. There were teachers who specialized in vocal music classes, as well as instrumental music classes. (Courtesy of Juanita Nava.)

Nell Hicks was the instrumental music teacher at Russell Public School. She once invited Deborah Tolefree (left) and Edith Eddens (right) to her San Lorenzo home for the weekend in order for them to practice without distraction for an upcoming concert. (Courtesy of Dorothy Tolefree-Babbitt.)

Although there was not a significant presence of families from the Pacific Islands in the Russell City area, some students of Puerto Rican descent came to live in California via the Hawaiian Islands and as a result had some experience in the culture. Teachers at the school reached out to the Hawaiian community in Hayward area in order to acquaint all of their students with the traditions and cultures of the Pacific Island region.

The Russell Public School graduating class of 1954 is pictured here: (first row) Sam Nava, Phillip Garcia, J. C. McClinton, Charles Bratton, and Eddie Posada; (second row) Sally Torres, Lou Ella Tourchette, Betty Reynolds, Stella Pomales, Joanne Huey, Adela Pomales, unidentified, Rosie Quiroz, and Angela Ordoñez; (third row) Phillip Ramirez, Daniel Dominguez, Verge Chattman, Elliot Watson, and Henry Timbers. (Courtesy of Sam Nava and Connie Anderson.)

Ministers from the churches in Russell City offered benedictions and invocations at the school graduation. Such celebrations were formal activities that involved the entire community. Programs engraved on luxurious card stock were issued to all who attended. For some students, this event marked the end of their formal education, as economic circumstance required them to enter the workforce. For other students, this event marked the beginning of their studies at Hayward Union High School, located 5 miles away in downtown Hayward. Sam Nava is escorting Rosie Quiroz at the head of this processional. A little behind is Charles Bratton, who is accompanying one of the girl graduates. (Courtesy of William Mette.)

Ralph Mendoza performs a vocal solo in this 1953 graduation ceremony. A graduation program from 1961 lists a processional whose musical accompaniment was the "Triumphal March" from Verdi's *Aida*. An instrumental interlude was performed by students of the violin, clarinet, and trumpet. An important indication of the ways in which teachers respected the diversity of the student body is that the song list they selected for the student vocalists included music derived from Swedish, Filipino, and African American traditions. Graduates from this 1953 class included Bevalen Brown (first row center), Cecilia Ordoñez, Faye Gullat (left rear), Jerry Reynolds, Manuel Alvarez, and Joe Clara (second row right). (Courtesy of William Mette.)

In 1953, valedictorian Jerry Reynolds (left) delivered his speech in English, and Manuel Alvarez (right) translated it into Spanish. The address was titled "Living the American Way." Graduation programs from other years indicate that sometimes two valedictorian addresses, as well as the requisite presentation of graduates and diplomas, were aspects of the grand ceremony. Boys who were graduating wore suits and ties, and the girls wore dresses of taffeta. The teachers assisted parents who could not afford the cost or didn't have the time to create the formal wear for their graduates. The school administration provided each graduate with a boutonnière or corsage. (Courtesy of William Mette.)

Four

CULTURAL EXPRESSIONS

Celebrities sometimes came to the small community of Russell City. Prizefighter Max Baer lived with his family for a few years on a nearby farm on Hesperian Boulevard. His sister Frances married Louis Santucci, and they operated a hog farm in Livermore. It is said that after he had become a successful boxer and was financially well off, Baer would travel down the dusty, pothole-filled Russell Road in a bright, shiny convertible headed for one of the clubs. Baer is shown here riding a horse in a 1940 Rowell Ranch Rodeo Parade, then held in Hayward.

One of two iconic images associated with Russell City (the other being the railroad station), the Russell City Country Club was known for its contradictory name and the reputation it had for attracting young talented blues musicians. Legend has it that renowned musicians such as Ray Charles, Big Mama Thornton, T-Bone Walker, and Jimmy McCracklin performed in Russell City.

Andrew Hill Jr. was co-owner of the Russell City Country Club located on Washington Street. Over the years, there may have been as many as four changes of ownership of the well-known landmark club. (Courtesy of Mildred Jean Hill-Eddens.)

Lowell Fulson was originally from Tulsa, Oklahoma, but moved to Oakland in 1943. While working at the shipyards by day, he performed by night in the area's small clubs, such as those found in Russell City. It is said that his guitar work "exemplified California rhythm and blues." He played with B. B. King, Eric Clapton, and Ray Charles. He was inducted into the Blues Hall of Fame in 1993 and nominated for a Grammy in 1996 for his album *Them Update Blues*. Lowell Fulson died in 1999. (Courtesy of the Mark Weber Jazz Collection, University of California, Los Angeles, Performing Arts Special Collection.)

When vocalist Dottie Ivory came to Russell City, people flocked to the clubs. Her full-throated voice was the favorite of many, and she was known to conclude her sets with the signature song "What a Difference a Day Makes." In her later years, she opened Dottie Ivory's Stardust Lounge located in the Fillmore District of San Francisco. This photograph depicts Dottie Ivory (right) in a period after the demise of Russell City.

Miss Alve's Club (also known as Miss Al's Club) was south of the Country Club, closer to Fourth Avenue, and it too was a popular destination point for people seeking good music, good food, and good company. This photograph includes Buster Brooks (fourth from left), who was called by some the "Mayor of Russell City."

Although the families who lived in Russell City were not affluent, they dressed with the flair that was required of Sunday church attendance and special occasions. This photograph of Loretta "Peaches" Connor Perry exemplifies the way in which some women brought a thoughtful attention to their mode of dress. The silk gardenia hairpiece, crystal drop earrings, and matching necklace offer a complete look of elegance. (Courtesy of Mildred Jean Hill-Eddens.)

Kenneth Eddens demonstrates how young men, too, paid attention to their style of dress. This blazer with white shirt, contrasting vest, and matching tie are traditional expressions of business dressing. The photograph on the arm of the sofa seems to indicate that this image was one in a series of shots, perhaps for a job application. (Courtesy of Mildred Jean Hill-Eddens.)

Robert Trotter was standing next to his car on Mission Boulevard between A and B Streets in downtown Hayward when this photograph was shot. Hayward and Oakland were destinations for young people seeking to develop broader social opportunities. (Courtesy of Mildred Jean Hill-Eddens.)

Appearance was important to the Figueroa brothers, who are, from left to right, James, Gilbert, and Faustino Jr. Gilbert bought his other brothers new suits whenever the occasion was warranted. In Russell City circles, the boys were known as "the Figs." (Courtesy of James and Priscilla Figueroa.)

Joe Cota worked as a chauffeur for the Santucci family. He was required to wear a suit to work, so he had this one custom made in 1939. He traveled the many miles to San José in order to have the finest of tailors create the suit. (Courtesy of Joe Cota.)

Mildred Jean Hill lived on Washington Street and later on Adams Street with her family while she was growing up in Russell City. Thomas Eddens lived on the southernmost edge of Washington Street. Youthful sweethearts, they married after graduating from Hayward Union High School. When Russell City was demolished, they moved to Oakland and rented a small room from Cleo Cannon, who was also displaced from Russell. (Courtesy of Mildred Jean Hill-Eddens.)

Carmen Liranzo (left) and her sister Mary (right) shared a common appreciation for stylishness, as did their friends. The Liranzo family was one of the largest landowners in Russell City. Mary died of leukemia at the age of 21, a tragedy that shook the family forever. Although Carmen was raised in the community, as an adult married to Albert Mateos, she moved to nearby Mt. Eden and raised their family on Depot Road near the intersection of Clawiter Road. (Courtesy of Linda Mateos Milistefr.)

Juanita Ramirez (right) and her sister Sally (left) were fortunate to have a mother, Beatrice, who was a talented tailor. She was able to create dresses such as those seen here so that her daughters would match the elegance of their dates. Sam Nava (right), Juanita's high school sweetheart and husband of almost 50 years, was her date for the prom this evening. (Courtesy of Juanita and Sam Nava.)

All children, especially boys, recall their first vehicle. This is Joel Arellano outside the family home in Russell learning to navigate the backyard. (Courtesy of Joe Cota.)

James Figueroa recalls with a mixture of pride and sorrow that in 1946 this was the first set of wheels, a tricycle, he was given. After posing for this photograph, he cycled out of the front yard and down the street only to drive right into one of the ever-present potholes and ruin the front wheel of his tricycle. It was bent out of shape, beyond repair, and what began as a happy moment ended sorrowfully. (Courtesy of James and Priscilla Figueroa.)

Harold Nygren (right) was well known for his motorcycle with sidecar as he drove the streets of Russell City. His wife, Anna Nielsen Nygren, holds their new baby Violet, as Harold readies them for a ride. (Courtesy of Karen Verili.)

Lou Ella Tourchette is seen here in 1960 working on her Harley-Davidson motorcycle while pregnant with her daughter Connie. Sam Nava, her Russell Public School classmate, describes Lou Ella as the "Babe Didrikson Zaharias" of her time and believes that had the families of Russell City been more affluent, Lou Ella might have been scouted and trained as a professional athlete. Even as she approaches her 50th year, Connie continues in her mother's tradition of motorcycling. (Courtesy of Connie Anderson.)

Some vehicles were intended for utilitarian purposes rather than pleasure driving. Richard Machado came to work at the Horat Dairy and fell in love with the farmer's daughter, Loretta Horat. They married in 1955. However, his second love was for his vehicles, including this truck used for hauling hay and other feed for the herds. (Courtesy of Loretta Horat Machado.)

This is a 1932 Chevrolet sedan that was a homemade motor home owned by the Figueroa family. The trunk of the car was cut out, and a flat bed with a wood top and walls were added. It was called "The Perrera" and known throughout Russell City by that name. Faustino used this car to make extra income by driving workers who did not own a car to their jobs. The men and canine members of the family are seen here, from left to right: James, the patriarch Faustino Sr. with Brownie, Faustino Jr. with Buchi, and Gilbert with Boots. (Courtesy of James and Priscilla Figueroa.)

Hermina and Edwina Nava pose with the family Plymouth in the front yard of their Russell home. (Courtesy of Joe Cota.)

Eight of the nine Nava children posed for this picture around the family car. Only seven kids are visible because Sam decided to be a big shot and sit behind the wheel of the car. If one looks closely, he can be seen in the driver's seat. (Courtesy of Sam and Juanita Nava.)

Although not yet old enough to drive when this photograph was taken, Marie Green, a young woman from Russell City, loved this car.

Figueroa brothers James (left) and Faustino Jr. (right) have always been proud car owners who in their spare time renovate older vehicles. James still attends Concours d'Elegance and displays his vintage automobiles. (Courtesy of James and Priscilla Figueroa.)

In their younger days, Rocky Ramirez (left), Frank Salazar (center), and Peter S. Ybarra (right) were aficionados of automobiles. Frank is seen here going through their pile of car photographs as the boys talk about variations on different models. (Courtesy of James and Priscilla Figueroa.)

José M. Cota and Elvira M. Cota, seen here, belonged to the Spanish-speaking Apostolic church located on the corner of Russell Road and Adams Street. The congregation later moved the church a few blocks away to Jefferson Street. Rev. Celso Moran was pastor of the Iglesia Apostolica de la Fe en Cristo Jesus, whose nucleus of parishioners lived in Russell City. When it closed in 1963, the congregation moved to Folsom Street in Hayward. (Courtesy of Joe Cota.)

Those in the choir of Iglesia Apostolica de la Fe included Sammy Cruz, Marta Zagaino, Esther Castillo, Alice Salazar, Mary Diaz, Betty Martinez, Paulita Vargas, Priscilla Figueroa, Nehomi Reymundo, Moises Varela, Elias Moran, Faustino Figueroa, James Figueroa, Joel Varela, Peter S. Ybarra, Manuel Ybarra, and Ruben Arellano. The congregation built the church located in Russell City out of adobe, which they handcrafted on-site. (Courtesy of James and Priscilla Figueroa.)

Some of the women in Russell City dressed in austere choir robes while others were festooned with fur wraps when they attended Sunday services. This photograph was taken in 1939. Magdalena Cota Leon (left) is with Hermina Arellano who is holding little Ruben Arellano. (Courtesy of Joe Cota.)

Jim Figueroa and Priscilla Varela were married on June 23, 1962, in the Iglesia Apostolica de la Fe en Cristo Jesus, and theirs was the last wedding held at the church. (Courtesy of James and Priscilla Figueroa.)

In 1928, the Reverend Climmie Tolefree was ordained as a Pentecostal minister in Pine Bluff, Arkansas. His family migrated to Oakland in 1940. In 1943, property was purchased in Russell City and Reverend Tolefree opened the doors to his first church in 1949. In 1959, he opened began another congregation on Third Avenue. After Russell City was demolished, he moved to Tracy and then Modesto, where he ministered to congregations until his retirement. (Courtesy of Dorothy Tolefree-Babbitt.)

Pictured is Rev. Climmie Tolefree (center) with various ministers and members of Russell City congregations at a religious reunion in Russell City. (Courtesy of Mildred Jean Hill-Eddens.)

Matriarch Octavia Tolefree wanted a family portrait to remember all of her children as youngsters when this photograph was taken in the early 1950s. Burnetta King, a neighbor child, was included. Shown are, from left to right, (first row) Burnetta King, Reverend Climmie, Dorothy, Octavia, and Deborah; (second row) Joseph, Jesse, Robert, Evell and Arthur Charles ("A. C."). (Courtesy of Dorothy Tolefree-Babbitt.)

Ruth Stone was a neighbor of the Pentecostal church when it was located on Third Avenue. Mrs. Stone is pictured here with, from left to right, Octavia, Deborah, and Rev. Climmie Tolefree. (Courtesy of Mildred Jean Hill-Eddens.)

The First Baptist Church of Russell City was well known for its vigorous ministry to those less fortunate. Members of the Green family were leaders of the church, which relocated to Kelly Hill in Hayward after the demise of Russell City. (Author's collection.)

Sports teams were common among the Russell City children. While there were a great many forms of unstructured play in the community, softball proved an excellent way to build cooperative behavior. Although the girls and boys were segregated in the organized sports that were sponsored, it is important to note that the girls had opportunities to develop their athletic skills during the 1930s when this photograph was taken. (Courtesy of Linda Mateos Milistefr.)

In many ways, organized athletics assisted in demonstrating the ways in which the children might learn from one another and assist each in developing camaraderie. This team photograph of boys' baseball is curious for the formal suits that some are wearing. The ethnic diversity of this 1930s-era team is also notable. The 1933 Russell City Ducks are remembered as having a winning year. Money for their uniforms was raised through the sale of tickets to the games: 35¢ for the gentlemen and 15¢ for the ladies. (Courtesy of Linda Mateos Milistefr.)

This 1954 softball game between teachers and pupils was one example of how the faculty worked with the community in developing the children in matters inside and outside the classroom. The scoreboard seems to indicate that the youthful energy of the students is prevailing. Joel Arellano (far left) and Juanita Ramirez (second from left) contemplate the pitching and fielding strategies of the opposition. (Courtesy of William Mette.)

This lively pickup game of coed street basketball includes Betty Reynolds, holding her baby brother while she cheers on the competition. Cecelia Ordoñez (in long pigtails) just made a shot, and Jerry Reynolds is under the basket going for the rebound. (Courtesy of William Mette.)

Pictured here are the Russell Public School champions of the 1946 Hayward Recreation Games.

After the construction of Sunset High School, Russell Public School students no longer attended Hayward High School. This is a basketball team from Sunset whose team members were from Russell City and the city of Hayward. Pictured are, from left to right, (first row) James Hill, Bobby Joe Harris, Jesse Gimeno, Roy Rideout, unidentified, John Ralls, and Ramon Quezada; (second row) unidentified, Carl Wesley, Joe Harris, David Ross, unidentified, Thomas Eddens, and unidentified. (Courtesy of Mildred Jean Hill-Eddens.)

Russell City girls marched as representatives of their Russell City Brownie Troop in an early-1950s Hayward Pet Parade that was held annually. From left to right, unidentified, Mabel Anthony, two unidentified, Judy Nuñez, Edith Eddens, and Blanche Green who all show good form. (Courtesy of William Mette.)

This "Sailor Dance" was performed in a 1949 talent show held at the Russell Public School. The dancers included Elinor ?, Mattie Sue ?, Lois Tavis, Mildred Porter, Sally Hernandez, Gina ?, Evelyn Brooks, and Virginia Gimeno. (Courtesy of Loretta Horat Machado.)

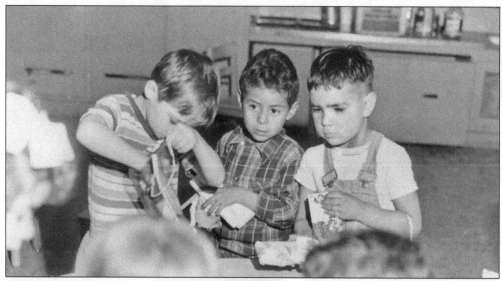

Dividing up the contents of a gift stocking handed out at a Christmas party sponsored by the Optimist Service Club in 1952 are Armando Saenz (center) and Miguel Magdaleno (right). (Courtesy of William Mette.)

Sisters Barbara and Muriel Manter posed in the Halloween costumes made by their mother, Christine Nielsen Manter. She crafted the little girls' outfits from tablecloths. When this photograph was taken during the 1920s, the sisters were headed for a Halloween parade, followed by a party at Andrew Johnson's General Store. The store had a dance hall in the rear where members of the community convened for celebrations. (Courtesy of Muriel Manter Knickerbocker.)

The Russell Halloween parade may have been a long-standing tradition in the community, but no one can say for sure when it began. Residents recall discussions about Halloween parades dating as far back as the early 1900s. It is thought that this particular Halloween parade being readied on the school grounds dates from the 1950s. (Courtesy of William Mette.)

In the 1950s, the costumed children marched down Russell Road and then back again to the school for a party. The roofs of the Russell Library and the Nygren home are visible over the tops of the trees in the background.

Norm Zimmerman was living with his mother, Ida Bach Zimmerman, in Pennsylvania when she heard of this spot on the San Francisco Bay that would be a perfect place to live, Russell City. The two moved there in May 1937. Norm and his mother lived there for one year, and he attended fourth grade at the Russell Public School. Although his time there was brief, he recalls good friends and plenty of playtimes in the surrounding fields. Norm (right) recalls that the lids the boys were using as shields may have come from washtubs. The home in the background is the Hansen residence, the family with whom Norm boarded, while his mother was working in the then faraway town of Berkeley. (Courtesy of Norm Zimmerman.)

During the 1940s and 1950s, photographers would travel door to door with a forlorn pony tempting little ones to pester their parents for a photo opportunity. The traveling photographers even came equipped with cowboy and cowgirl outfits. It appears that James Figueroa prevailed when he asked his parents for the money it cost. (Courtesy of James and Priscilla Figueroa.)

Lou Ella Tourchette stands by a gas pump at her family's business on Russell Road. With a six-shooter in each hand, she looks as though she could use some playmates. (Courtesy of Connie Anderson.)

Sisters Loretta (left) and Tina (right) Horat play around on the safety light near the railroad crossing on Russell Road in 1953. (Courtesy of Loretta Horat Machado.)

Family swing sets were not common in the backyards of Russell City homes. However, the Horat children were fortunate that their parents invested in some play equipment for them and their friends. From left to right, Holly and Albert Jr. Horat with three unidentified friends paused for this 1953 photograph. The Horat home was not located at the family dairy but at 25094 Monroe Street in the center of Russell City. (Courtesy of Loretta Horat Machado.)

In spite of having the fancy swing set, the Horat children were able to create playthings from just about any object; just witness, from left to right, Albert Jr., Bill, and Gloria play with an unidentified friend in the wine barrels. Perhaps the barrels came from a still that was said to be run out of someone's backyard in Russell City. (Courtesy of Loretta Horat Machado.)

Former residents speak with pride about the success they enjoyed as children in play and later as adults at work in their cross-cultural, interracial relationships. This young duo has the cowgirl and boy outfits complete with fancy boots. (Courtesy of William Mette.)

Willie Hill was pumping iron in the family backyard on Adams Street when this photograph was taken. Was he wearing the jaunty derby or was that an addition for the photograph? (Courtesy of Mildred Jean Hill-Eddens.)

Bob Keropian was the physical education teacher at Russell Public School and is recognized by many of the former students as being the key to the development of their abilities as athletes. This photograph is of students who were practicing for an upcoming competition in 1953. (Courtesy of William Mette.)

This is the Russell Public School Traffic Patrol Squad for 1949. They travelled to a school in the Central Valley to compete in a regional competition where they demonstrated their skills as a team. Some of the members of that year's group included Loretta Horat, Beverly Thomas, Mack Porter, Albert Green, Lee Otis Thomas, Christina Horat, Lupe Salazar, Ethel Ann Matusic, Estelle Lewis, Hellen Torres, and Capt. Billy Franklin. (Courtesy of Loretta Horat Machado.)

For many of the students in Russell City, the school photograph days were important because they provided one of the few opportunities to document themselves as young people. This montage of high school portraits was created by Mildred Jean Hill and includes, from left to right bottom to top: (first row) Rusty Kinnerman and three unidentified students; (second row) Laura Torres, Elias Moran, Rosetta Hill, and Eddie Woods; (third row) Armando Cisneros, Dorothy Tolefree, Freddie Rodriguez, and an unidentified student; (fourth) Earlene Ross, James "Sonny" Hill, an unidentified student, and Ezra "June" Rideout. (Courtesy of Mildred Jean Hill-Eddens.)

Five

DISPLACEMENTS AND CIRCULATIONS

During the 1950s, the City of Hayward planned to acquire the land of Russell City for an industrial park, and by 1964, the residents and businesses were entirely removed through eminent domain proceedings. Because the area was unincorporated, it was under the jurisdiction of Alameda County. The County Redevelopment Agency reported that they would need to relocate 205 families, 33 individuals, 13 businesses, and 7 churches in their acquisition and preparation of the 200 acres they were acquiring for subsequent sale to the City of Hayward.

Numerous arsons occurred while the eminent domain proceedings were underway. Residents were fearful to leave their homes, worried that they might be burned while they were away at work or running errands. The caption on this photograph notes that the fire taking place was the sixth one in a week in the community.

As the number of fires grew, so did the ire of the residents, church congregations, and business owners who felt that their requests for assistance in organizing themselves into a municipality had gone unheeded for decades. Minutes from a meeting held by the Eden Council for Civic Unity in June 1953 indicate that residents were trying to plan for the construction of infrastructure such as utilities, including a water and sewage system, which had never been provided to the community.

To compound matters, a fire began on an open lot that had stored hundreds of tires on-site. The fire burned for days and spread to homes next door, burning down the Hill family home as well as others' residences. (Courtesy of Mildred Jean Hill-Eddens.)

This rubble was all that remained of the Hill family home after the fire. (Courtesy of Mildred Jean Hill-Eddens.)

After the demise of Russell City, the many residents, church congregations, and businesses were scattered. Some people, like Ruby Tolefree-Echols, weren't willing to part with the close-knit friendships they had developed with one another. She spoke with Henry "Billy" Garron about getting people together, and the two founded the annual reunion picnic. Ruby Tolefree-Echols died in 2002. (Courtesy of Dorothy Tolefree-Babbitt.)

Russell City reunion picnic cofounder Henry "Billy" Garron still attends the picnics, but Sam and Juanita Nava now perform the coordination. Kennedy Park in Hayward, near the land that was formerly Russell City, is the site of the annual gathering. Invitations are mailed out, but it is well known among the former residents that this is the place to be on the Sunday before Labor Day. (Author's collection.)

"The Pioneers" was the title given to the oldest living former residents of Russell City, who are, from left to right, Novaline Simmons, Octavia Tolefree, Buster Brooks, Cleo Cannon, and Chauncey Pryor, who attended each of the early reunion picnics. (Courtesy of Dorothy Tolefree-Babbit.)

There are some who attend every year. Joe Green cooks the best barbecue, and Novaline Simmons provides her quiet compliments about his cooking. (Author's collection.)

Ernesto R. Nava attends every year. He moved his family to Russell City in the 1930s, and from there, he built a highly successful plastering company. His son Sam continues the business. Ernesto R. Nava takes pride in the fact that he is a son of Francisco "Pancho" Villa, the great Mexican land reform revolutionary. (Courtesy of James and Priscilla Figueroa.)

Other regulars to the reunion picnic include, from left to right, James Figueroa, Daniel Diaz, and Henry Diaz. (Courtesy of James and Priscilla Figueroa.)

Sam Nava brings a map to the reunion picnic that people use to identify their homes, churches, and businesses. No matter how often people attend, the map is always a useful way to reaffirm some memory of the community. (Courtesy of James and Priscilla Figueroa.)

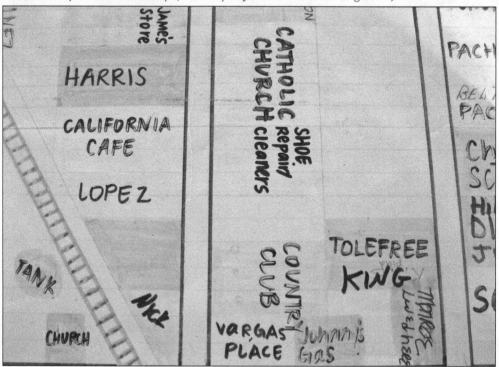

The level of detail provides persons unacquainted with the town a sense for how the community organized itself, the number of businesses that were present, the quantity of churches, as well as the diversity of the families who lived in Russell City. (Courtesy of James and Priscilla Figueroa.)

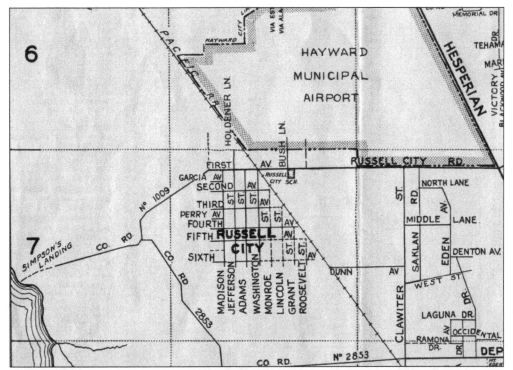

A map from the 1950s provides some details on how the streets corresponded to official public landmarks. Please note that the landing has undergone a name change. Mt. Eden is the neighborhood in the lower left corner.

"The city may be gone, but the memories live on" is often repeated by the former residents of Russell City. Although many bring their grandchildren to the reunion picnic, the elders quietly wonder if the tradition will endure with future generations. Recent reunion picnic attendees shown here are, from left to right, Willie Hill, Geraldine Brooks, Henry Diaz, Paul Lopez, and Zenobia Kimble Breaux. All of them lived in Russell City and remember it with great fondness. (Courtesy of James and Priscilla Figueroa.)

127

Visit us at
arcadiapublishing.com
....